DEDICATIONS

To the little girl who once cried when she felt helpless and couldn't save them all, I dedicate my work in animal rescue to those individuals who believed, and currently believe in me: my husband, my MFP Family, mi familia, my mamita Barbara. And to the heart of my girls who were once just like me, little girls wishing to save the world and today they rock and fight to save hundreds of animals neglected by humanity. Lastly, every single rescue that ever crossed my life—those still with us and those over the rainbow bridge where we will meet again one day. Love you all. THANK YOU!

— Heydi Acuna

For all the rescue dogs and cats in my life, you make my world bright and beautiful.

— Precious McKenzie

Bright and Beautiful

THE STORY OF THE MERCY FULL PROJECT

WRITTEN BY **PRECIOUS MCKENZIE**

ILLUSTRATED BY **SHELBY KOEHLER**

BEALU BOOKS

new voices for curious readers

Your purchase of *Bright and Beautiful* supports The Mercy Full Project's community outreach and animal rescue.

Thank you,
Luana Mitten
CEO, BeaLu Books

Main Text of the Story and Back Matter
Copyright 2025 by Precious McKenzie

Illustrations
Copyright 2025 by Shelby Koehler

ISBN Hardcover: 978-1-962981-04-0
ISBN Paperback: 978-1-962981-05-7

Library of Congress Control Number: 2024934492
Publisher's Cataloging-in-Publication Data is on file with the publisher.

Written by: Precious McKenzie
Illustrated by: Shelby Koehler
Edited by: Luana K. Mitten
Book cover and interior design by Tara Raymo • creativelytara.com

Printed in the United States of America
March 2024

BeaLu Books
Tampa, Florida

www.BeaLuBooks.com

In Bogotá,
there are many
BRIGHT and
BEAUTIFUL things....
the blossoms, the birds, the buildings,
the music, the people.

5

But most of all,
　　Yeyi's grandmother.

Yeyi's grandmother
　　cooked for the family,
　　　and sewed their clothes,
　　　and mended their bruised knees.

She walked Yeyi to school and to church.

She taught her about love
   and kindness
      and respect.

When she saw someone lonely,
   sad, or sick, she helped.
Yeyi's grandmother
   made Bogotá
BRIGHT and
   BEAUTIFUL.

Because sometimes Bogotá was not

BRIGHT and BEAUTIFUL.

Sometimes there lurked hunger and hopelessness.

People forgot,
forgot about the animals who wandered the square
bone-thin, broken, bruised.
Who had no home, no food,
no one to love them.

There was just one man
who shared his bits of food
with the ragged dogs.

13

"Why does no one help them?" Yeyi asked. Grandmother took her hand and said, "Mi amor, sometimes people choose to look away because they cannot bear the pain."

But, that day, near the church,

    Yeyi chose not to look away.

She filled a bucket with cool water.

    She filled a dish with scraps of food.

She took the small amount

    of money from her pocket

      and gave it away.

The dogs wagged their tails.

The man smiled.

Everything became

BRIGHT and

BEAUTIFUL.

Yeyi went through
    the streets of Bogotá.
She kept bread in her pockets
    that she fed to the stray
    cats and dogs.

She taught children
how to be kind to animals.
From the greatest to the smallest,
Yeyi cared for them all.

One day, a broken dog followed
      Yeyi and her mother home.
But they did not have room
      for a large dog in the city.
She begged her mother
      to let the dog stay with them,
for a short time, until he was well again.

Yeyi fed him and built a small house
      for him with a bed and a blanket.
She healed him
      and loved him.

When he was strong enough,
Yeyi found him a happy home on a farm
in the country, with room to play.
Everything became
BRiGHT and BEAUTiFUL.

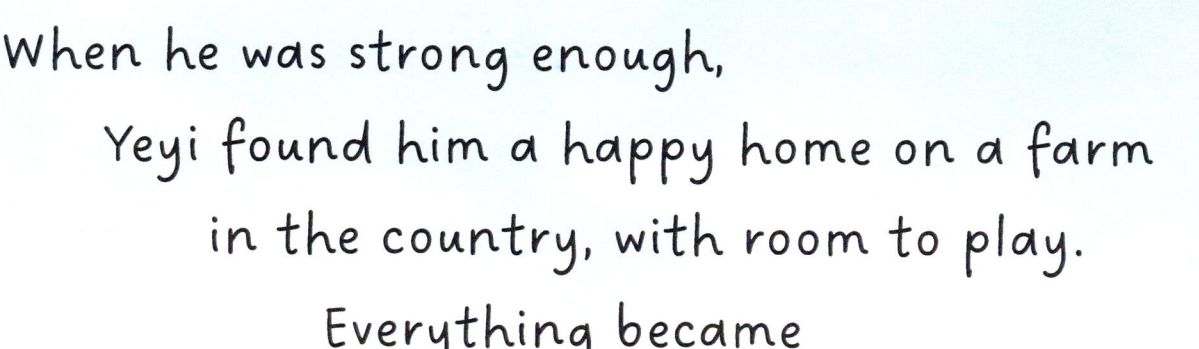

As Yeyi grew and traveled the world,
she saw many good people
who loved their animals.

But she saw many people
  who did not and she saw
many animals who needed help.
  She found many sad animals,
many hurt and sick ones, too.

  She took them, one by one,
    to the animal hospital
  where they received care,
    and medicine, and bandages.

Then, Yeyi taught them
how to trust again,
how to love again,
and how to play again.
She saw happiness
and hope fill their eyes.
All things were

BRIGHT and
BEAUTIFUL again.

But, Yeyi needed to do more.
She wanted a world where
no animals were hurt or hungry.

So Yeyi, with the help
of many friends and loved ones,
built a home full of mercy,
where she brings
lost and broken animals.

901

Mercy Full Project
Empathy - Kindness - Love
Animal Rescue & Nonprofit
Organization Center

WWW.MERCYFULLPROJECTS.ORG

Where they find foster homes
    to care for them,
where those animals are loved and fed,
    where those animals will find
forever families to love.

All thanks to the friends
who share their time and love,
Because it all began with Yeyi,
who learned how to make the world
BRIGHT and BEAUTIFUL,
once upon a time, on the streets of Bogotá.

THE MERCY FULL PROJECT
AND ANIMAL RESCUE INFORMATION

All across the world there are animal rescue organizations. These organizations are made up of individuals who love animals and who want to help them.

Animal rescue organizations do all kinds of work. Some, like the Mercy Full Project, help cats and dogs find their forever homes. Others, like the Seal Rescue Ireland, rescue and rehabilitate injured wild seals.

People who work in animal rescue organizations say that their work can sometimes be scary, dangerous, and even sad. They work long hours, trying to help animals and give them the medical care they need. They know, though, that not all animals survive, but they do their best for each and every one of them, always hoping that each animal can go on to live a long, happy life.

At the Mercy Full Project, in Tampa, Florida, Heydi Acuna and her team, focus on finding forever homes for cats and dogs. This book is based off Heydi's childhood and her dream of helping animals. Now, Heydi's dream is coming true. Heydi and her volunteers say the best part of their work is when families adopt their new best friends. Get involved and learn more about the Mercy Full Project at https://mercyfullprojects.org/.

ABOUT THE MERCY FULL PROJECT FOUNDER

Heydi Acuna, or Yeyi, was born and raised in Bogota, Colombia. After graduating high school in 2008, Heydi got her first job working for her mom's friend at a veterinary clinic. But Heydi dreamt of being a veterinarian and started vet school in 2009. When Heydi's dad was able to help her immigrate to the United States as a refugee, she left vet school without hesitation. Heydi moved to Tampa, Florida, with her dad. And Tampa is so very lucky she did!

Following the American dream, Heydi learned English and pursued a career as a preschool teacher for over five years, followed by working in corporate America. Even though she had left behind her dream of being a veterinarian in Colombia, she was growing as a person, volunteering with many organizations to help animals in the community, and all the while, her vision of her own animal rescue was taking shape in her mind.

In 2019, she married Nash. And together, after just ten years in the United States, they started Mercy Full Project (MFP), a nonprofit animal rescue. With the help of many individuals, Heydi and Nash grew MFP from Heydi's car to their own facility in the heart of downtown Tampa. Heydi is quick to say the only reason she can do all this work is because of the individuals who follow her mission—fosters, volunteers, and donors—to make the world a better place for voiceless animals in need. And make Yeyi's dream of a bright and beautiful world a reality.

Thank you, Heydi! The world is bright and beautiful for many animals and families (including my own) because of your work.

xo
Luana & Ollie (a MFP puppy)

HOW KIDS CAN HELP

Animal shelters and rescue organizations need lots of things. You can help!

1. If your family is able, you may foster a cat or dog until it can find its forever home.

2. Many shelters have programs like "Take a Dog for a Day" or "Take a Pet Home for the Weekend." These programs allow families to bring an animal home from the shelter for a short period of time. The animal has a chance to relax, play, and have fun until they find their own family.

3. Contact your local rescue organization. They may accept donations such as cat food, cat litter, dog food, shampoo, treats, towels, and toys.

4. You might make blankets and toys for animals. These toys help them feel loved and safe.

ABOUT THE AUTHOR

Precious McKenzie is a children's book writer who lives in Montana with her family, including her rescue cats and dogs. She is the author of *Cinder Yeti*, *Ruffian*, *Infestation*, *Nest*, and many other books for kids.

To learn more about Precious, visit preciousmckenzie.com.

ABOUT THE ILLUSTRATOR

Shelby Koehler is an artist and illustrator, currently based in Raleigh, North Carolina, where she lives and makes art with her cat Dini. Find her portfolio and more at shelbykoehler.com.